Jul 2017

AFRICAN AMERICANS IN THE MILITARY

MARCIA AMIDON LUSTED

TITLES IN THIS SERIES

AFRICAN AMERICANS IN THE MILITARY

MARCIA AMIDON LUSTED

MASON CREST
PHILADELPHIA

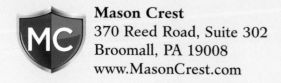

Mason Crest
370 Reed Road, Suite 302
Broomall, PA 19008
www.MasonCrest.com

Printed and bound in the United States of America.

CPSIA Compliance Information: Batch #MBC2012-9. For further information, contact Mason Crest at 1-866-MCP-Book.

First printing
1 3 5 7 9 8 6 4 2

Library of Congress Cataloging-in-Publication Data

Lüsted, Marcia Amidon
African Americans in the military / by Marcia Amidon Lusted.
    p. cm. — (Major Black contributions from emancipation to civil rights)
Includes bibliographical references and index.
Audience: Age 12.
ISBN 978-1-4222-2379-6 (hbk.)
ISBN 978-1-4222-2392-5 (pbk.)
1. United States—Armed Forces—African Americans—Juvenile literature.
2. United States—History, Military—Juvenile literature. I. Title.
E185.63.L87 2012
305.896'073—dc23
                                        2011051948

Publisher's note: All quotations in this book are taken from original sources, and contain the spelling and grammatical inconsistencies of the original texts.

TABLE OF CONTENTS

INTRODUCTION

Dr. Marc Lamont Hill

It is impossible to tell the story of America without telling the story of Black Americans. From the struggle to end slavery, all the way to the election of the first Black president, the Black experience has been a window into America's own movement toward becoming a "more perfect union." Through the tragedies and triumphs of Blacks in America, we gain a more full understanding of our collective history and a richer appreciation of our collective journey. This book series, MAJOR BLACK CONTRIBUTIONS FROM EMANCIPATION TO CIVIL RIGHTS, spotlights that journey by showing the many ways that Black Americans have been a central part of our nation's development.

In this series, we are reminded that Blacks were not merely objects of history, swept up in the winds of social and political inevitability. Rather, since the end of legal slavery, Black men and women have actively fought for their own rights and freedoms. It is through their courageous efforts (along with the efforts of allies of all races) that Blacks are able to enjoy ever increasing levels of inclusion in American democracy. Through this series, we learn the names and stories of some of the most important contributors to our democracy.

But this series goes far beyond the story of slavery to freedom. The books in this series also demonstrate the various contributions of Black Americans to the nation's social, cultural, technological, and intellectual growth. While these books provide new and deeper insights into the lives and stories of familiar figures like Martin Luther King, Michael Jordan, and Oprah Winfrey, they also introduce readers to the contributions of countless heroes who have often been pushed to the margins of history. In reading this series, we are able to see that Blacks have been key contributors across every field of human endeavor.

Although this is a series about Black Americans, it is important and necessary reading for everyone. While readers of color will find enormous purpose and pride in uncovering the history of their ancestors, these books should also create similar sentiments among readers of all races and ethnicities. By understanding the rich and deep history of Blacks, a group often ignored or marginalized in history, we are reminded that everyone has a story. Everyone has a contribution. Everyone matters.

The insights of these books are necessary for creating deeper, richer, and more inclusive classrooms. More importantly, they remind us of the power and possibility of individuals of all races, places, and traditions. Such insights not only allow us to understand the past, but to create a more beautiful future.

Photograph of General Colin Powell in 1989, the year he became the first African-American officer to serve as chairman of the Joint Chiefs of Staff. In this position, Powell was the main military adviser to the president of the United States.

1

A RECORD OF SERVICE

In 1989, President George H. W. Bush named General Colin Powell chairman of the Joint Chiefs of Staff. Powell was the first African American to receive this honor. He had already served as the national security advisor for President Ronald Reagan. He had attained the highest rank in the United States Army—four-star general—and had commanded more than a million soldiers. Now he would be in charge of all the military leaders giving advice to the president. In his announcement, President Bush said, "[General Powell] will bring leadership, insight, and wisdom to our efforts to keep our military strong and ready, prepared to defend our security and to safeguard the peace."

Soon after President Bush's announcement, Powell gave a speech in which he said that his new job would not have been possible "without the sacrifices of those black soldiers who served this great nation in war for over 200 years." African-American soldiers had fought bravely in every war Americans had ever waged. Their service started with the conflict that secured the nation's independence: the Revolutionary War.

FIGHTING THE REVOLUTION

By 1770, the American colonies simmered with tension. Many colonists believed that British policies infringed on their rights, and they were determined to resist. In Boston on the cold night of March 5, 1770, passions boiled over into deadly violence. British soldiers opened fire on a mob of rioting colonists, killing five. The first to fall was a black man, a former slave named Crispus Attucks. He and the other victims of what came to be called the Boston Massacre were considered martyrs of the Patriot cause.

On April 19, 1775, the first shots of the Revolutionary War were fired at Lexington and Concord. African-American Patriots stood shoulder to shoulder with their white neighbors that day. Two months later, black Patriots fought at Bunker Hill, one of the bloodiest battles of the entire war.

In these early battles, the valor of African Americans was unquestioned. Yet not all Americans wanted black soldiers in the army. Slaveholders feared that the cause of liberty might inspire an armed slave uprising. At the outset of the war, about 2.5 million people lived in the American

After the Battle of Bunker Hill in 1775, one soldier was singled out for a special commendation signed by the American commander, Colonel William Prescott, and other officers. Salem Poor, whom the commendation praised as a "brave and gallant soldier," was a free black man from Massachusetts. Poor also fought at Saratoga and Monmouth, two important American victories.

colonies. Of that number, about 500,000 were black slaves. In addition, there were perhaps 40,000 free blacks in the colonies. In July 1775, shortly after taking command of the Continental Army, General George Washington issued orders that banned the recruitment of all African Americans—free or enslaved.

British leaders and their American supporters, called Loyalists, saw an opportunity. They knew that slavery was an issue that divided Americans. The British offered freedom to any slave owned by a Patriot master who fought on their side. Thousands of slaves fled their masters and joined the British. Many were not treated especially well. The British had the African Americans do the backbreaking work of building roads and forts. Some were even sent as slaves to other British colonies in the Caribbean.

The First Rhode Island Regiment

Rhode Island was the smallest American colony. During the Revolutionary War, it had trouble finding enough men to fill the ranks of its two regiments. So a regiment composed predominantly of blacks—the first such unit in the Continental Army—was raised. Known as the First Rhode Island Regiment, it had about 225 to 250 men and was commanded by a white colonel.

The First Rhode Island was untested in combat, and most of its soldiers were recent recruits, when the unit was called on to cover the Continental Army's retreat during the Battle of Rhode Island on August 29, 1778. Over the course of four hours, the men held their position, ferociously repulsing repeated attacks by crack British regiments.

Later, the First Rhode Island would fight with distinction in New Jersey and New York. At the close of the war, their commander would praise his men for "faithfully persevering in the best of causes, in every stage of service, with unexampled fortitude and patience."

Fighting with the Swamp Fox

Major fighting in the American Revolution shifted to the southern states in 1778. That year, British forces captured the important city of Savannah, Georgia. In May 1780, they seized the large port city of Charleston, South Carolina. Three months later, the British crushed the American army at the Battle of Camden in South Carolina. It appeared that all of the southern states might fall into British hands.

But effective resistance came from an unlikely source: a small group of ragtag fighters led by an officer named Francis Marion. Marion waged a guerrilla war. His men struck the British with surprise attacks and night-time raids. Then they quickly retreated into the swamps of South Carolina, where British forces were unable to find them. These tactics earned Marion the nickname "the Swamp Fox."

Many members of Marion's band were African Americans. They had greater immunity than whites to diseases common in the swamp, such as malaria and yellow fever. As a result, Marion's black soldiers were able to fight even when most of his white soldiers were sick.

Francis Marion wanted freedom for his state and his country. But like most southerners at the time, he was not interested in freedom for black Americans. He owned slaves before and after the war. One of them, named Oscar, cooked for Marion's unit.

The American general Francis Marion invites a captured British officer to share a meal with his men in this painting. Marion's slave Oscar is shown at the lower left preparing sweet potatoes.

By late 1775, the Continental Army faced a critical shortage of soldiers. On December 31, General Washington reversed his earlier decision and ordered that free blacks be allowed to serve in the army. Many free blacks from the North joined the Patriot cause. Later, black slaves were permitted in the Continental Army as well. Some even fought as substitutes for their white masters. Often, but not always, these slaves received their freedom in return.

By 1777, African Americans were serving in almost every regiment of the American military. Overall, during the American Revolution, about 5,000 African Americans fought on the Patriot side. They saw action in every major campaign. During the Yorktown campaign in 1781, an estimated 25 percent of the army was black.

One black soldier, Doctor Harris, later spoke about his experiences during the war:

> I served in the Revolution, in General Washington's army. . . . I have stood in battle, where balls, like hail, were flying all around me. The man standing next to me was shot by my side—his blood spouted upon my clothes, which I wore for weeks. My nearest blood, except that which runs in my veins, was shed for liberty. My only brother was shot dead instantly in the Revolution.

When the Revolutionary War ended in 1783, the United States had gained its independence. However, very few African Americans gained their own freedom. Most blacks continued to be slaves. By 1790, the number of slaves in the United States had grown to more than 700,000.

— Did You Know? —

In the spring of 1781, an African American claiming to be a runaway slave reached British lines in Virginia. James Armistead soon gained the trust of Lord Cornwallis, the British commander. Cornwallis recruited him to spy on the Americans. But Armistead was actually spying for the Americans. He passed false information to Cornwallis while relaying British plans to the Continental Army. Armistead's efforts helped lead to the American victory at the Battle of Yorktown.

THE WAR OF 1812

The postwar American army was small. By 1789, it had only about 800 men. Three years later, a law was passed that prevented blacks from enlisting. Still, some African Americans continued to serve on warships of the U.S. Navy.

In 1807, an American warship called the USS *Chesapeake* set out from Norfolk, Virginia. The ship was headed to the Mediterranean for patrol duty. It never got there. Soon after leaving port, it was stopped by a British warship, the HMS *Leopard*. The *Leopard* fired its cannons at the *Chesapeake*, killing three Americans and wounding 18 others. The American ship was not able to defend itself and had to surrender.

The British boarded the ship, supposedly to look for deserters from the Royal Navy. They took three black sailors with them. This incident outraged Americans. President Thomas Jefferson first placed an embargo, or ban, on trade with Britain. When the British continued to stop American ships and force Americans to serve in the Royal Navy, the United States declared war in 1812.

Blacks and whites work together in this painting of the Battle of New Orleans.

When the war began, many African Americans joined the U.S. Navy and fought in battles against British ships. Commodore Isaac Chauncey commanded the American naval force on Lake Ontario. His ship had 50 black sailors, and he considered many of them among his best men. "I have yet to learn," Chauncey noted, "that the color of a man's skin . . . can affect a man's qualifications or usefulness."

During the War of 1812, the U.S. Army's official policy was to keep blacks out of the ranks. In Louisiana, however, African Americans were permitted to serve in militia regiments. When General Andrew Jackson was preparing to defend New Orleans from a British attack, he made a point of recruiting black soldiers. "As sons of freedom, you are now called upon to defend our most inestimable blessing," Jackson said.

> ═ Did You Know? ═
>
> One of the African Americans who fought with Andrew Jackson during the Battle of New Orleans—the last major battle of the War of 1812—was Jordan Noble. He was only 13 when he signed up as a drummer boy. Noble was a free black who also fought during wars against the Seminole Indians and in the Mexican-American War.

To every noble-hearted, generous freedman of color volunteering to serve during the present contest with Great Britain, and no longer, will be paid the same bounty, in money and lands, now received by the white soldiers of the United States . . . and will not, by being associated with white men in the same corps, be exposed to improper comparison or unjust sarcasm.

Jackson later told his black troops in the Louisiana Battalion of Free Men of Color, "I expected much from you . . . but you surpass my hopes." They were heroes, at least until the war was over. Then, once again, they and all other African Americans were banned from serving in the U.S. Army.

Black soldiers had served America well during its struggles to become an independent country and ward off British aggression. They would play a much larger role in a war that ripped apart the United States itself. In this war, the stakes for black soldiers were even higher.

African-American soldiers in action near Dutch Gap, Virginia, in 1864. In all, more than 186,000 blacks fought for the Union during the Civil War.

FIGHTING FOR FREEDOM

2

The American Civil War tore the country apart. The war raged from 1861 to 1865, claiming more than half a million lives. The underlying cause of the conflict was slavery. Many people living in the North were against the slave system. However, the South's plantation economy depended on slave labor.

In 1860, Abraham Lincoln was elected president. Lincoln opposed slavery, and the Southern states proceeded to secede, or withdraw, from the United States. They formed their own government. It was called the Confederate States of America, or simply the Confederacy.

Fighting between the Confederacy and the U.S. government, or Union, broke out in April 1861. The outcome of the Civil War would determine the status of blacks in the United States.

Only a week after the start of the war, Jacob Dobson, a free black man from Washington, D.C., sent a letter to the U.S. secretary of war. "I desire to inform you," Dobson wrote, "that I know of some 300 of reliable colored free citizens of this city, who desire to enter the service for the defense of the city."

From the beginning of the war, African Americans were eager to fight for the North. But as earlier, they found that they were not welcome in the military. President Lincoln initially did not allow blacks to enlist, because

After escaping from slavery, Frederick Douglass (1818–1895) became a famous activist. He spoke and wrote eloquently about the injustice of slavery.

he worried that many Northerners would object. "Colored men were good enough to fight under Washington, but they are not good enough to fight under [Union general] McClellan," Frederick Douglass, a free black author and abolitionist, noted bitterly. "They were good enough to help win American independence, but they are not good enough to help preserve that independence against treason and rebellion." Douglass predicted that whichever side first enlisted blacks would prevail. Fortunately for the Union, the Confederates also would not permit African Americans in their ranks.

THE LOUISIANA REGIMENTS

In July 1862, the U.S. Congress passed legislation that provided for the enlistment of African Americans into the Union army and navy. In New Orleans, which Union forces had captured three months earlier, about 1,000 free blacks formed a regiment called the First Louisiana Native Guard. Soon runaway slaves were flocking to New Orleans and seeking to enlist in the unit.

At first, the Union military commander in New Orleans, General Benjamin F. Butler, balked at allowing slaves to serve. But eventually Butler changed his mind, and two more regiments of the Louisiana Native Guard were formed.

It was a widely held belief—among officers and enlisted men in the Union and Confederate armies alike—that blacks could not make great soldiers. Blacks were said to lack the courage and intelligence to excel on the battlefield. For the most part, the Native Guard regiments supported the regular Union army. They built roads and army camps and gathered supplies. In May 1863, however, the First and Third Louisiana Native Guard units took part in an attack on the Confederate fort at Port Hudson. Thousands of black soldiers were killed or wounded when they charged the fort. Eventually, the Confederates surrendered. General Daniel Ullman, commander of the all-black units, praised their bravery. "They were exposed to a terrible fire and were dreadfully slaughtered," Ullman said. "All who witnessed these charges agree that their conduct was such as would do honor to any soldiers. The conduct of these regiments on this occasion wrought a marvelous change in the opinion of many former sneerers."

On June 7, 1863, two black regiments of the Union army took part in a different battle, at Milliken's Bend, Louisiana. They defended a supply area from attack by thousands of Confederate troops. It was not a big battle, but it was important. If the supply area at Milliken's Bend had been captured, the Confederates would have been able to get supplies to Vicksburg, an important city on the Mississippi River. Thanks in part to this determined defense by African-American soldiers, Union troops were able to capture Vicksburg on July 4. This was one of the North's biggest victories of the war.

The bravery shown by these African-American soldiers from Louisiana helped convince Abraham Lincoln and other American leaders that blacks should have the chance to serve in their country's military. Soon the government began recruiting black soldiers. By the end of the Civil War, more than 186,000 black soldiers would fight in the Union army.

THE 54TH MASSACHUSETTS

One of the most famous black regiments to fight for the Union was the 54th Massachusetts Colored Infantry. It was formed in Boston in March 1863. One thousand black men joined the regiment. The commanding officers were white.

The first major battle for the 54th Massachusetts came on July 18, 1863. The regiment attacked Fort Wagner, a strong Confederate base in

This painting shows African-American soldiers of the 54th Massachusetts Regiment assaulting the Confederate stronghold at Fort Wagner, South Carolina, in 1863. Sergeant William Carney is pictured holding the American flag. The story of 54th Massachusetts was told in the 1989 movie *Glory*.

South Carolina. A week earlier, white Union troops had attacked the fort. They had been turned back with heavy losses. The soldiers of the 54th Massachusetts charged bravely. A few reached the top of the fort's wall. However, the Confederate position was too strong. After hand-to-hand fighting, the black soldiers were driven back. Of the 600 who participated in the heroic assault, 272 were killed, wounded, or captured.

Early in the fight, a black sergeant named William H. Carney rescued the regiment's flag after the soldier holding it was killed. Carney carried the flag during the assault against the Confederate lines. He held it at the top of the fort's wall, to inspire the Union soldiers to come forward. When Confederates forced the troops to retreat, Carney went with them. A white soldier from another brigade offered to carry the heavy flag for him. Carney refused, saying, "No one but a member of the Fifty-fourth should carry the colors." Despite being wounded, Carney never allowed the flag to fall. For his actions, he would eventually receive the Medal of Honor. This is the most prestigious award an American soldier can earn.

The 54th Massachusetts failed to capture Fort Wagner. But the soldiers' bravery in battle convinced many doubters that black soldiers could fight as well as whites.

UNEQUAL TREATMENT

Although African-American soldiers had shown that they could fight, they were still not treated equally. The lowest-ranking white soldiers in the Union army were paid $13 a month. They received pay raises as their rank increased. Black soldiers were paid $7 a month, regardless of how many promotions they received or how long they stayed in the army.

Abolitionists argued that the pay difference was unfair. And as the war dragged on, the Union army faced a growing need for more men— white or black. In June 1864, the U.S. government finally agreed to pay all soldiers equally.

Black soldiers also faced unequal treatment at the hands of the enemy. White Union soldiers who were captured would be sent to prison camps, where they were supposed to receive food and medical care and be treated humanely. But, according to a

The uniform this black soldier is wearing indicates he served in an artillery unit.

law passed by the Confederate Congress in 1863, any African-American soldier who was captured could be executed or enslaved. White officers serving with black troops also faced execution.

Blacks and the Confederate Army

In the Confederacy, the notion of having black soldiers in the ranks seemed unthinkable, at least during the first years of the war. But the South did use slave labor to support the army. Slaves built forts and roads. They hauled supplies.

As the war dragged on, however, the Union's manpower advantage became more decisive. Increasingly, the South struggled to replace its casualties with fresh recruits. In 1864, a Confederate general named Patrick Cleburne proposed a solution: permit slaves to be soldiers. Any slave who served in the Confederate army, Cleburne said, should be granted freedom for himself and his family at the end of the war.

Confederate leaders were horrified by Cleburne's proposal. Jefferson Davis, the president of the Confederate States of America, called the idea treason. Slavery was the basis of the Southern way of life. Preserving it was the reason the South was fighting the war.

By the spring of 1865, however, the Confederacy was near collapse. The South's top general, Robert E. Lee, said that the only hope left was to allow blacks to fight. "We must decide whether slavery shall be extinguished by our enemies and the slaves be used against us, or use them ourselves at the risk of the effects which may be produced upon our social institutions," Lee declared in a letter to the Confederate Congress. "My own opinion is that we should employ them without delay."

Lee was so highly esteemed that his argument carried the day. On March 13, 1865, the Confederate Congress passed a law allowing blacks to serve. A black unit was hastily organized in Richmond. But only a few dozen men were enlisted, as Lee surrendered his army at Appomattox Courthouse less than a month later.

African-American soldiers stand guard outside the White House during the Civil War.

One of the worst Confederate atrocities occurred on April 12, 1864. That day, about 1,500 Confederates led by General Nathan Bedford Forrest attacked Fort Pillow, a Union base in Tennessee. About half of the fort's 600 defenders were black. After fierce fighting, the defenders of Fort Pillow surrendered. Forrest's men then bayoneted and shot black soldiers who had thrown down their weapons. Only 65 black soldiers survived.

The Confederates may have hoped this massacre would stop blacks from fighting. But it had the opposite effect. After the Fort Pillow Massacre, black troops fought extra hard to avenge their murdered comrades. "Remember Fort Pillow" became a popular battle cry.

* * *

By the end of the Civil War, blacks made up nearly 10 percent of the Union army. Nearly 38,000 had lost their lives in the conflict, and many more were wounded. Eighteen African Americans were awarded the Congressional Medal of Honor. No one could deny that black soldiers had given their last full measure of devotion to the Union cause.

African-American Spies in the Civil War

Spying played a significant role in the outcome of the Civil War. The ability of Northern leaders to gather information about Confederate plans gave them an advantage on the battlefield. Many brave African-American men and women worked as spies for the Union cause.

One spy who provided valuable information was William A. Jackson. He was a servant in the home of Jefferson Davis, the Confederate president. There, he was able to listen to Davis discussing military matters with his top generals. In May 1862, Jackson escaped to the North. The information he gave about Confederate plans and army positions was so significant it was immediately sent to the War Department in Washington, D.C.

Mary Touvestre was a freed slave who lived in Portsmouth, Virginia. She worked as a housekeeper for a Confederate naval engineer. He was busy converting a captured ship, the USS *Merrimack*, into an ironclad warship called the CSS *Virginia*. Touvestre stole plans for the new ship and took them to Washington, D.C. When leaders of the U.S. Navy learned about the dangerous new Confederate ship, they sped up their own program to build an ironclad, the USS *Monitor*. The *Monitor* was ready in time to fight the *Virginia* before it could do major damage to the Union fleet of wooden ships.

Information provided by Mary Touvestre caused the U.S. Navy to speed up its program to develop an ironclad warship. The USS *Monitor* was constructed just in time to counter the threat posed by the Confederate ironclad CSS *Virginia*.

Harriet Tubman is best known for her work helping slaves escape to freedom on the Underground Railroad. She also worked as a spy for the Union. She sneaked into South Carolina and gathered information about the Confederate army from black men and women living there. In June 1863, she led 300 Union soldiers on a raid against a Confederate outpost on the Combahee River in South Carolina. About half of the soldiers were African Americans. The Union raiders set fire to supplies and buildings so the Confederate army couldn't use them. They also freed more than 700 slaves.

Harriet Tubman

John Scobell was a freed slave with a talent for acting and a flair for disguises. Allan Pinkerton, the head of the Union Intelligence Service, hired Scobell to go behind enemy lines and spy. Scobell worked with two of Pinkerton's best white agents. Disguised as a servant, he sought out blacks in Virginia who knew about Confederate forts and troop positions. Scobell provided valuable information in 1861 and 1862.

Robert Smalls was a slave who worked steering ships through the harbor at Charleston, South Carolina. In 1861 and 1862 he was working

aboard the CSS *Planter*, a Confederate ship. One night in May 1862, when the white captain and crew members were on shore, Smalls and a few other black sailors took control of the ship. They sailed through the Confederate defenses and turned the ship over to the Union Navy. Because of his knowledge of the harbor, Smalls was able to give the Union commander important information about the Confederate defenses. Smalls continued to serve with the Union Navy, and in 1863 became the first African American to command an American warship. After the war, he served in the U.S. Congress.

Robert Smalls

These soldiers of the Ninth Cavalry are taking part in a raid against Apaches in Texas during the 1870s. After the Civil War ended, four regiments of African-American soldiers were sent west to protect settlers during the Indian Wars from the 1860s to the 1890s.

3

BUFFALO SOLDIERS

T he U.S. military continued to permit African Americans to serve in the years after the Civil War. But black soldiers did not enjoy equal status with their white counterparts. The segregated regiments in which they served were often poorly supplied. They received old equipment and weapons. Black cavalry units made do with aged horses. Black regiments did not even receive regimental flags of their own. A flag was an important part of a regiment's identity. Most black regiments created and sewed their own flags.

Black army regiments were also likely to draw the most demanding deployments. For instance, they traveled to the western frontier, where conditions were harsh and the forts often had no proper buildings. As one white commander reported, "The troops are good, but their accommodations are wretched." In addition to poor conditions, the black regiments had an even bigger problem ahead: the Indian Wars.

FIGHTING INDIAN WARS

The Indian Wars—a series of conflicts between the U.S. government and Native Americans—were at their bloodiest in the years following the Civil War. During that period, a flood of white settlers poured onto the Great Plains and into the Southwest. They sought new opportunities and land.

Buffalo soldiers of the 25th Infantry at Fort Keogh, Montana, in 1890. Some of the soldiers in this photo are wearing buffalo robes.

But, of course, the land was already occupied by Indian tribes. The Indians fought to protect their land and way of life. The U.S. Army was now called on to protect white settlers as they moved westward. The black regiments posted on the frontier shared that duty.

The Native Americans actually gave the black soldiers the nickname that they would keep. They called them "Buffalo Soldiers," possibly because their black curly hair looked like a buffalo's coat. The African-American soldiers liked the name. They liked to think of themselves as being as stubborn and steady as buffalo. The buffalo was a sacred animal to the Plains Indians. It was an honor to share that name, so the name Buffalo Soldiers stuck. One army unit, the Tenth Cavalry, even added a buffalo to its regimental flag.

There were six original regiments of Buffalo Soldiers, but that number was soon reduced to four. They were the Ninth and Tenth Cavalry, and the

24th and 25th Infantry. The Buffalo Soldiers recruited another group of men to help them keep order on the frontier. The new army recruits, who would serve as scouts for the Buffalo Soldiers, were descendants of African Americans and Seminole Indians who had settled in Texas.

The Buffalo Soldiers were involved in many battles during the Indian Wars. From 1867 to 1890, they fought against tribes like the Cheyenne, the Sioux, and the Arapahoe. The Native Americans often carried out small raids on isolated ranches or small traveling groups. Many of the Buffalo

African Americans and West Point

After the Civil War, many African Americans were eager to serve in the U.S. Army. To become a commissioned officer, however, it was necessary to attend the United States Military Academy at West Point.

In 1870, James Webster Smith became the first African American ever accepted into West Point. But Smith never graduated. He endured four years of harassment from white classmates before being dismissed for academic failures.

The second black cadet at West Point was Henry O. Flipper. Born a slave in Georgia, Flipper entered the U.S. Military Academy in 1873 as a 17-year-old. Though completely shunned by his fellow cadets, he managed to graduate. In 1877, he was commissioned a second lieutenant in the U.S. Army. Flipper's military career was brief, however. In 1881, he received a dishonorable discharge for "conduct unbecoming an officer." Most historians believe the charges were a product of racial bias. And during the 1970s, an army review board officially overturned Flipper's dishonorable discharge.

Another African American, Charles Young, graduated from West Point in 1889. Young eventually rose to the rank of colonel. He became the first black to command a regiment in the regular army. But after Young, West Point would not have any more black graduates until 1932.

= Did You Know? =

In 1878, the Buffalo Soldiers were called on to help quell violence in Lincoln County, New Mexico Territory. They pursued, but were unable to catch, a young gunman who called himself William H. Bonney. History knows him better as Billy the Kid.

Soldier units spent their time trying to find Indian camps or chasing raiders who had attacked settlers.

OTHER JOBS

Indian fighting was by no means the only responsibility of the Buffalo Soldiers. They also guarded stage-coaches and supply wagons. They escorted the mail. They helped build new roads. They defended against the outlaws who roamed the western frontier. And they performed these tasks with distinction.

Once, in a remote area of Arizona, 11 members of a Buffalo Soldier regiment were protecting an army wagon carrying money to pay soldiers. Suddenly, a group of bandits attacked. The firefight that erupted was fierce. But the African-American troops heroically repulsed the bandits. "I served in the infantry during the entire Civil War and served in 16 major battles," declared the army paymaster in charge of the wagon, "but I never witnessed better courage, or better fighting than shown by those colored soldiers."

The Buffalo Soldiers also helped rescue stranded settlers and their animals during severe weather. They delivered supplies to remote settlements. In 1881, after a brutal winter in the Dakota Territory, hundreds of settlers were on the verge of starvation. When government relief supplies ran low, members of a Buffalo Soldier regiment even used some of their own pay to buy more supplies for the desperate settlers.

NEW ASSIGNMENTS

By 1890, the United States had won the Indian Wars, and most of the defeated tribes were living on reservations. The Buffalo Soldiers had participated in more than 200 battles. Members of these African-American regiments had been awarded 18 Medals of Honor for bravery under fire.

Troopers of the Tenth Cavalry on the hunt for Native Americans. The white officer in the center is Colonel Benjamin Grierson (1826–1911). A hero of the Civil War, Grierson organized and commanded the Tenth Cavalry after the war. He believed that black soldiers were as good as white troopers—a belief that made him unpopular with other white officers.

After a quarter-century of service, the Buffalo Soldiers had earned the respect of just about everyone. The Indians they had fought respected them. Soldiers in white regiments respected them. Officials in Washington, D.C., respected them.

The Buffalo Soldiers would be called on again to fight for their country. This time it would not be on American soil.

Soldiers of the 24th Infantry Regiment march to the ships that would carry them to Cuba during the Spanish-American War, 1898.

4

WARS AROUND THE WORLD

In the mid-1890s, a struggle for independence broke out in Cuba. The island, located less than 100 miles from Florida, had been a possession of Spain since the voyages of Christopher Columbus. Most Americans sided with the Cuban revolutionaries, especially after a brutal crackdown by Spanish forces.

In January 1898, the U.S. government sent a battleship to Cuba's Havana Harbor. The ship, the USS *Maine*, was supposed to protect American citizens and business interests on the island. But on the night of February 15, 1898, an explosion destroyed the Maine and killed more than 250 crew members. The cause of the blast was unclear. But American newspapers blamed Spain and called for war.

IN CUBA AND MEXICO

In April 1898, Spain and the United States declared war on each other. And four regiments of the Buffalo Soldiers were among the first U.S. troops sent to fight in the Spanish-American War.

The Buffalo Soldiers would fight under Colonel Theodore (Teddy) Roosevelt. Roosevelt commanded an all-white regiment of volunteer caval-

ry. They were known as the Rough Riders. At Las Guásimas, the first battle of the Spanish-American War, the Rough Riders tried to take a heavily
defended position. The attack stalled under heavy fire from Spanish sharp-
shooters. But then two Buffalo Soldiers cavalry regiments joined the battle. After a 90-minute fight, the Americans took the Spanish position. A
newspaper reporter named Stephen Bonsal witnessed the action at Las
Guásimas. He wrote about the important role played by the black troopers. "They were no braver certainly than any other men in the line," Bonsal
said, "but their better training enabled them to render more valuable services than the other troops engaged."

Charles Young (1864–1922) was the
first African American to achieve the
rank of colonel in the U.S. Army. He
is pictured while commanding a
detachment of black troops in
Mexico, 1916.

U.S. forces soon prevailed in Cuba. The
fighting there formally ended on July 17,
1898. The Rough Riders and Teddy
Roosevelt had won great fame. For his
part, Roosevelt was quick to acknowledge
the contributions of the black soldiers. He
called them "brave men, worthy of respect.
I don't think any Rough Rider will ever for-
get the tie that binds us to [them]."

After the Spanish-American War, Teddy
Roosevelt returned to civilian life. In 1901,
he became president of the United States.

The Buffalo Soldiers, meanwhile, had
other missions to complete. One was an
expedition into northern Mexico. This time
the enemy was Mexican revolutionary
Pancho Villa. In March 1916, Villa led his
forces across the U.S. border. They
attacked the town of Columbus, in the
New Mexico Territory. Black troopers were
among the 4,800-man U.S. force dispatched to pursue and punish Villa. They
fought in the rugged desert lands of north-

ern Mexico. By January 1917, Villa's troops had been dispersed, and most of the American soldiers were withdrawn from Mexico.

By this time, a much larger war was raging in Europe. The four Buffalo Soldiers regiments would not see action in that conflict. But a new group of black soldiers would.

WORLD WAR I

The First World War—known at the time as the Great War—exploded in August 1914. It pitted the Central Powers against the Allied Forces. The Central Powers were led by Germany, the Austro-Hungarian Empire, and the Ottoman Empire. The Allies included Great Britain, France, and Russia. In the first years of the war, the United States remained neutral. But in April 1917, it entered the conflict on the side of the Allies.

About 4.5 million Americans volunteered or were drafted into the armed forces to fight in the Great War. This included more than 350,000 African Americans. Two new black combat divisions were organized. Most of their officers were also African American. This was a milestone in U.S. military history.

These African-American troops served with a French infantry unit, 1918.

Still, African-American soldiers were not treated as the equals of their white comrades. And for the most part, they were not treated very well. They trained as hard as whites. But black units were denied combat roles. In part this was because of fears that white soldiers would refuse to fight alongside African Americans. So most black soldiers ended up in the engineering, signal, or medical corps. Black labor battalions did heavy work such as unloading ships, digging trenches, and clearing battlefields of destroyed equipment and dead bodies.

Eventually, some African-American units did get the chance to prove their mettle on the battlefields of World War I. By late 1917, France was suffering a serious shortage of able-bodied men. To deal with this problem,

The Houston Riot

In 1917, a 600-man detachment from the 24th U.S. Infantry—an African-American regiment—was assigned to guard a new army camp being built near Houston, Texas. White troops would be trained there before going to European battlefields.

Many of the black troops, who came from posts in the western United States, were pleased that they would be stationed near Houston. The city had a large black population. But racial tensions flared as soon as the black soldiers arrived. The soldiers found themselves harassed by Houston's white police force. White workers building the camp also treated the soldiers with contempt.

Tensions boiled over after a fight between Houston police officers and black military police. On the night of August 23, 1917, about 100 soldiers from the 24th Infantry grabbed their rifles and marched into Houston. A riot erupted, during which the black soldiers fired into a crowd of Houston police officers and civilians. At least 15 people were killed and 12 wounded in the riot. Only one of the dead was black. It was the first time in American history that a race riot claimed more white lives than black lives.

French leaders requested that African-American units be placed under French command. John J. Pershing, the top U.S. general, agreed. He transferred four black regiments, including the 369th Infantry, to the French. In April 1918, the soldiers of the 369th took their place in the front-line trenches. They would remain at the front until the end of the war—191 days in all. This was longer than any other American unit spent at the front.

The French soldiers alongside whom they fought dubbed the members of the 369th Infantry the "Men of Bronze." The enemy Germans called them the "Harlem Hellfighters." Both nicknames reflected admiration and respect. In more than six months of fighting, the 369th never surrendered an inch of ground. Not a single one of its men was ever captured.

Two members of the Harlem Hellfighters, Corporal Henry Johnson and Private Needham Roberts, won special acclaim. On the night of May 14, 1918, Johnson and Roberts were the only soldiers manning an isolated outpost when a German patrol attacked. Grenades wounded both men. Needham was unable to stand. But when 20 or more German soldiers tried to storm the outpost, the two African Americans refused to yield. Johnson received more than a dozen wounds in the ferocious fight that followed. But he killed or wounded at least a dozen Germans and prevented the retreating survivors from dragging Roberts away. For his heroism, Johnson became the first American awarded France's Croix de Guerre ("Cross of War"). Roberts also received the medal.

> ══ *Did You Know?* ══
>
> The Harlem Hellfighters also made great music. The 369th Infantry's regimental band was made up of some of the finest musicians in the eastern United States. The band became famous for introducing jazz music to Europe.

Johnson and Roberts were not the only African-American soldiers recognized for their heroism in World War I. Nor was the 369th Infantry Regiment the only black unit that distinguished itself in combat. In September 1918, another black regiment under French command, the

This painting shows the 369th "Harlem Hellfighters" Infantry Regiment advancing at Sechault, France, on September 29, 1918, during the Meuse-Argonne offensive. Members of the famous African-American regiment are also pictured on page 7 of this book.

371st Infantry, was engaged in tough fighting in France's Champagne province. On the 28th, Company C of the 371st was ordered to take Hill 188—a high, wooded hill near the town of Ardeuil. Under heavy fire, the African-American troops advanced steadily up the hill. As Company C was closing in, the German soldiers emerged from their trenches. They threw down their weapons and raised their arms as if they were surrendering. But this was a trick. When the American troops approached to take them prisoner, the Germans leaped back into the trenches and opened fire with machine guns. More than half of Company C's men, including the officers, were cut down.

A corporal named Freddie Stowers quickly took over. Stowers crawled toward the German lines, calling for the rest of the men to follow. He directed the troops in silencing the German machine guns. Then he led a charge at the German trench lines. Stowers was felled by two bullets. But he urged his men to continue fighting. They did, overrunning the German position. Stowers, however, died.

The Black Swallow of Death

World War I was the first war to make use of airplanes. At first, all of the pilots were white. At the time, it was widely believed that African Americans did not have the intelligence or physical skills to fly airplanes. However, this assumption was soon proved wrong.

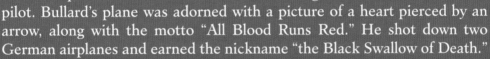

Eugene Jacques Bullard, born in Georgia in 1894, had traveled to Europe to escape racism in the United States. He eventually settled in France.

At the outbreak of World War I, Bullard joined the French Foreign Legion. He fought in several battles as an infantry soldier and was seriously wounded. No longer able to serve in the infantry, Bullard learned how to fly. In 1917, he joined a French squadron. He was the first black fighter pilot. Bullard's plane was adorned with a picture of a heart pierced by an arrow, along with the motto "All Blood Runs Red." He shot down two German airplanes and earned the nickname "the Black Swallow of Death."

Bullard applied for a transfer to the United States Army Air Corps when America joined the war. The transfer was denied. Bullard later had a fight with a French officer because of a racial comment. As a result, he was returned to the infantry.

Bullard remained in France after the war. He died in 1961.

Over the next week, the 371st Infantry Regiment formed the tip of a big offensive in Champagne. The regiment fought bravely. Nearly half of its men were killed or wounded in the offensive. Still, the 371st captured four towns, took many German prisoners, and secured critical weapons and supplies.

The heroism of the 371st was widely recognized. France bestowed the Croix de Guerre on 123 members of the regiment. One officer received the Legion of Honor, France's highest decoration. The United States awarded the Distinguished Service Cross to 22 members of the 371st.

Sadly, Freddie Stowers was overlooked. The corporal who died leading his company on Hill 188 did not receive any honors until 73 years after his death. In 1991, President George H. W. Bush awarded him the Medal of Honor. The citation for the medal said, "Inspired by Stowers' selfless heroism and bravery, Company C continued its attack against incredible odds, contributing to the capture of Hill 188 and causing heavy enemy casualties."

AFTERMATH

In July 1919, the Allied Forces staged a huge parade in Paris to celebrate their victory in the Great War. Not a single black soldier marched with the U.S. Army units.

At the conclusion of the war, many African-American units were given tedious or hazardous jobs. Some prepared military equipment to be shipped back to the United States. Others loaded ships. Some cleared minefields of unexploded mines, which was very dangerous work. Others were responsible for removing the bodies of U.S. servicemen from temporary graveyards so that they could be reburied in military cemeteries. And once they were ready to return home, African-American soldiers often found themselves restricted to the least comfortable areas of transport ships.

Many black soldiers had expected that their service in the Great War would lead to greater racial equality in American society. They were disappointed. The contributions of African-American soldiers to the war effort were mostly overlooked. Black veterans returning to their homes in the United States found the same discrimination and second-class status they had faced before the war.

5

"STRONG ENOUGH TO WHIP THEM BOTH"

On December 7, 1941, Japanese forces launched a surprise attack on the U.S. naval base in Pearl Harbor, Hawaii. The attack drew the United States into World War II, which had been raging for more than two years.

As had been the case during World War I, many blacks thought service to their country could—and should—be accompanied by greater equality at home. "We call upon the president and Congress to declare war on Japan and racial prejudice in our country," read an editorial published in the black-owned *Pittsburgh Courier*. "Certainly we should be strong enough to whip them both."

The issue of racism was especially visible during World War II. Nazi Germany, Japan's ally, proclaimed that there was a "master race." This supposed race—which the Nazis called the Aryans—was made up of white, blue-eyed, blond-haired people of northern European ancestry. In the Nazi view, everyone else was racially inferior, though in varying degrees. Blacks, the Nazis said, were among the lowest of the races. The Nazis would persecute and murder millions of people in the name of their racial ideas.

When the United States declared war on Nazi Germany, Japan, and other nations that sided with them, hundreds of thousands of African

Americans answered the call to serve their country. Again, however, they were expected to serve in segregated units. For many African Americans, this was simply unacceptable. "The Negro population will not silently suffer the discrimination and abuse which were heaped upon Negro solders and officers in World War I," declared Charles H. Houston, an African-American veteran of the First World War, in a letter to the U.S. secretary of war. "We urge you to remove all racial barriers to service in all branches of the army."

Houston's plea fell on deaf ears. The U.S. armed forces would remain segregated throughout World War II. But once again, black units would

Dorie Miller

Arguably, the first American hero of World War II was a black man. Doris "Dorie" Miller was a cook aboard the USS *West Virginia*. The battleship was at anchor in Pearl Harbor at the time of the Japanese attack of December 7, 1941. With his ship on fire, Dorie Miller carried his wounded captain to safety. Then he manned an antiaircraft gun. Miller had no training with the weapon, as it was against navy regulations for blacks to be taught how to fire antiaircraft guns. Still, Miller shot down four Japanese planes.

For his heroism, Miller became the first African American awarded the Navy Cross. In November 1944, he was killed in action in the Pacific.

Dorie Miller receives the Navy Cross from Admiral Chester W. Nimitz, commander of the U.S. Navy's Pacific Fleet.

Major James A. Ellison returns the salute of Mac Ross of Dayton, Ohio, as he passes down the line during review of the first class of African-American pilot cadets at the U.S. Army Air Corps flying school in Tuskegee, Alabama, 1941.

prove in combat that they were just as good as their white counterparts.

THE TUSKEGEE AIRMEN

The airfield in Tuskegee, Alabama, trained pilots for the war. In 1941, the Tuskegee Institute, as it was called, received its very first class of 13 black cadets. Congress had passed the Civilian Pilot Training Act in 1939 to prepare pilots in case the United States went to war. It allowed colleges and universities to send students for flight training. A previous public law had been enacted to create more schools for flight training. Because of pressure from the black community, this law included the creation of at least one school for black pilots.

The Tuskegee Institute gave blacks the chance to show that they could be successful combat pilots. Five cadets graduated in 1942. They included Benjamin O. Davis, Jr. A graduate of West Point, he was the son of the only black general in the U.S. Army. Because of his experience, Davis became the commander of the 99th Pursuit Squadron. By October of 1942, Davis had enough qualified pilots to fill his squadron. The Tuskegee Airmen, as they would be called, were ready for action.

In July of 1943, the Tuskegee Airmen faced their first combat. Off the

coast of Sicily, they were attacked by German fighter planes. The pilots of the 99th performed well, with Lieutenant Charles Hall shooting down an enemy fighter. The *Birmingham News* published an account of the fight:

> When the screaming P-40 Warhawks, piloted by the first Negro fighter pilots in the history of the world, roared though the Mediterranean skies to aid an allied offensive . . . the Tuskegee trained pilots faced their acid test and came through with flying colors to prove that they had the necessary mettle to fly successfully in combat.

The Tuskegee Airmen would have a distinguished flying record throughout World War II. In all, they flew more than 15,000 sorties (individual

Five pilots of the 332nd Fighter Group pose in front of a P-51 fighter plane on the airfield at Ramitelli, Italy. Pictured are (left to right) Lt. Dempsey W. Morgran, Lt. Carroll S. Woods, Lt. Robert H. Nelron Jr., Capt. Andrew D. Turner, and Lt. Clarence P. Lester.

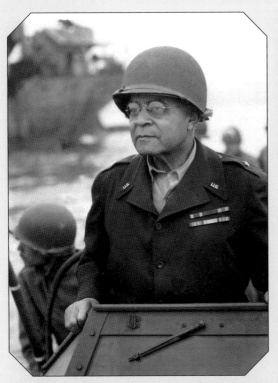

In 1940, Benjamin O. Davis Sr. (left, 1877–1970) became the first African-American to earn the rank of general in the U.S. Army. Davis Sr. spent 50 years in the army; he is pictured in France in 1944. His son Benjamin O. Davis Jr. (1912–2002) was commander of the Tuskegee Airmen during World War II. He flew more than 60 missions during the war, saw action as a jet pilot in the Korean conflict, and eventually became the first African-American general in the U.S. Air Force.

missions) and were credited with destroying more than 260 enemy aircraft. Tuskegee Airmen were awarded 95 Distinguished Flying Crosses.

THE 761ST TANK BATTALION

The 761st Tank Battalion was another African-American combat group. The battalion, nicknamed the Black Panthers, landed in France in October 1944. The Black Panthers would be engaged in 183 days of continuous operations. They fought under the famously tough American general George S. Patton.

Before the 761st went into battle for the first time, Patton addressed the unit. "Men, you're the first Negro tankers to ever fight in the American Army," he said.

> I have nothing but the best in my Army. I don't care what color you are as long as you go up there and kill [the enemy]. Everyone has their eyes on you and is expecting great things from you. Most of all your race is looking forward to your success. Don't let them down and . . . don't let me down!

The Black Panthers did not let Patton down. Their motto was "Come out fighting!" And they lived up to that motto. At the end of the war, the battalion received many citations for distinguished service. One soldier, Ruben Rivers, received the Medal of Honor. Rivers was killed in combat in 1944.

THE GOLDEN THIRTEEN

During World War II, significant numbers of African Americans finally had the chance to become officers in the U.S. Army, albeit in segregated units. The U.S. Navy offered fewer leadership opportunities for blacks.

At the outset of the war, African-American sailors were limited to being stewards or messmen, who served other sailors meals. In 1942, the navy began training black sailors for other roles, but they were still restricted to certain positions. It wasn't until 1943 that the navy agreed to start training African Americans to be officers. The first class of 16 officer candidates began training in 1944. They were only given half the usual amount of training. But when they took their exams, they received the highest scores ever recorded.

Thirteen of these men were commissioned as officers. They were known as the "Golden Thirteen." They were the first step to creating a more equal navy.

= Did You Know? =

Jackie Robinson was one of the original members of the 761st Tank Battalion, though he never saw combat. In 1947, Robinson broke baseball's "color barrier," becoming the first African-American to play in the Major Leagues since the late 1800s.

The first group of African-American officers in the U.S. Navy came to be known as the "Golden Thirteen." Pictured are (top, left to right) John Walter Reagan, Jesse Walter Arbor, Dalton Louis Baugh, Frank Ellis Sublett, (middle) Graham Edward Martin, Charles Byrd Lear, Phillip George Barnes, Reginald E. Goodwin, (bottom) James Edward Hair, Samuel Edward Barnes, George Clinton Cooper, William Sylvester White, and Dennis Denmark Nelson.

EXECUTIVE ORDER 9981

By September 1945, World War II was finally over. The United States and its allies had won decisively. Unfortunately, black World War II veterans returned home to face more racial discrimination.

The U.S. armed forces remained segregated. President Harry Truman decided to change that in 1948. On July 26 of that year, Truman issued Executive Order 9981. It ended segregation in the armed forces. "It is hereby declared to be the policy of the President," the executive order said, "that there shall be equality of treatment and opportunity for all persons in the armed services without regard to race, color, religion, or national origin."

For the first time since the Revolutionary War, African Americans would be allowed to serve on equal footing with white soldiers. Before long, the new policy would be put to the test in another war.

Black Marines

On June 1, 1942, the United States Marine Corps decided to accept African Americans into its ranks. For 167 years, the Marines had excluded blacks. The first African American to enlist in the Marine Corps was a man named Howard Perry. He was part of the initial group of 1,200 African-American volunteers.

Black Marines trained and were deployed in segregated units until 1949. That year, after initially resisting President Truman's desegregation order, the Marine Corps began training black and white recruits together.

STILL SERVING

By 1950, President Truman's order to desegregate the military was just beginning to take effect. Little by little, black servicemen—including officers—were being incorporated into units in all branches of the armed forces. Nevertheless, many units remained mostly white. And many units remained all or mostly black. Among white servicemen, there was still considerable opposition to desegregation.

In June 1950, North Korean forces launched a massive invasion of South Korea. A communist country, North Korea received support from the Soviet Union and China, two large communist nations. The United States quickly dispatched troops to help South Korea repel the invasion.

The first American units to arrive were poorly equipped and not well trained. Many retreated at the first contact with the enemy. These included the mostly black 24th Infantry Regiment. Bigots, repeating the old and thoroughly disproved lie, would say this showed that African Americans made poor soldiers. In truth, black and white U.S. troops alike were routed during the first months of the war. The North Korean forces nearly overran all of South Korea.

But by September 1950, U.S. forces had launched a successful counterattack. Nearly three more years would pass before the fighting finally ended in stalemate. By that time, the U.S. military was fully integrated.

(Top) A machine gun crew made up of black and white soldiers with the 2nd Infantry Division watches North Korean troops, November 1950. (Bottom) Despite President Truman's 1948 executive order, desegregation of the military was not immediately accomplished. The U.S. Army continued to have some all-black regiments until 1954. This photo shows members of the 24th Infantry Regiment moving up to the battle line, June 1950.

As with previous conflicts, African Americans proved their bravery, skill, and willingness to sacrifice during the Korean War. About 600,000 blacks served, and an estimated 5,000 were killed in combat. Several African Americans received the Medal of Honor.

In the wake of the Korean War, the idea that blacks should serve as equals in the U.S. armed forces was no longer controversial. As Lieutenant Herbert M. Hart, a white U.S. Marine in Korea, explained, "It doesn't make any difference if you are white, red, black, green or turquoise to the men over here."

VIETNAM

The next major conflict in which the United States became involved was the Vietnam War. The war, fought to prevent communist forces from taking control of South Vietnam, became highly unpopular among the American public. More than 58,000 American soldiers would lose their lives in the war.

Between 1965 (when large numbers of U.S. troops were first sent to Vietnam) and 1969, African Americans and other minorities bore the brunt of the war. That is because men of draft age (18–25) could avoid service through deferments. One of the most popular of these was enrollment in college. Overall, African Americans and other minorities were poorer than white Americans. Many could not afford college tuition. Thus they were drafted into the army in large numbers. The situation led the civil rights leader Martin Luther King Jr. to refer to Vietnam as "a white man's war, a black man's fight."

Yet for many African Americans, military service was an attractive option. The military offered the chance to earn decent wages. It also offered the opportunity for career advancement based on merit. Despite the successes of the civil

= Did You Know? =

Twenty black soldiers were awarded the Medal of Honor for their service in Vietnam.

rights movement, prospects for many black people were not so good in civilian life. In the 1960s, racial discrimination was still widespread in American society. During the Vietnam War era, African-American servicemen reenlisted at twice the rate of their white counterparts.

In 1969, the United States ended the system by which men could avoid the draft through college deferments. Instead, a lottery system based on day of birth was introduced. This spread the burden of fighting in Vietnam more broadly across race and class. The last U.S. troops were withdrawn from Vietnam in 1973.

A UNITED MILITARY

After the Vietnam War, the draft was discontinued, and an all-volunteer U.S. military was created. African Americans continued to enlist at high rates.

The Preacher

Milton Olive was a member of the 173rd Army Airborne Brigade. During the Vietnam War, this brigade was involved in many especially fierce battles. Olive was nicknamed "Preacher" because he liked to quote from the Bible. On October 22, 1965, Olive used his own body to cover an enemy grenade and save four of his comrades. He was killed instantly. His commanding officer later said, "It was the most incredible display of selfless bravery I have ever witnessed."

Olive was awarded the Medal of Honor. It was the first one given during the Vietnam War. The citation read, "Through his bravery, unhesitating actions, and complete disregard for his safety, he prevented additional loss of life or injury to the members of his platoon. Pfc. Olive's extraordinary heroism, at the risk of his life above and beyond the call of duty, are in the highest traditions of the U.S. Army."

The city of Chicago named a park and a college after him.

In 1975, Daniel "Chappie" James (1920–1978) became the first African-American four-star general in the U.S. Air Force. A fighter pilot trained at the Tuskegee Institute during World War II, he also flew combat missions during the wars in Korea and Vietnam.

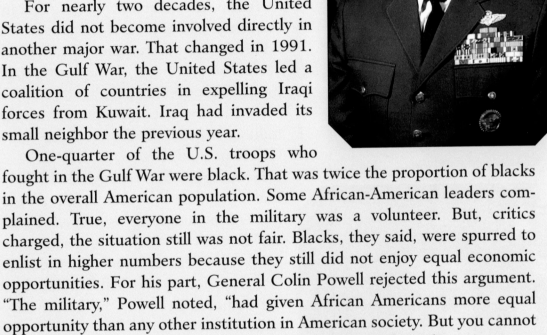

For nearly two decades, the United States did not become involved directly in another major war. That changed in 1991. In the Gulf War, the United States led a coalition of countries in expelling Iraqi forces from Kuwait. Iraq had invaded its small neighbor the previous year.

One-quarter of the U.S. troops who fought in the Gulf War were black. That was twice the proportion of blacks in the overall American population. Some African-American leaders complained. True, everyone in the military was a volunteer. But, critics charged, the situation still was not fair. Blacks, they said, were spurred to enlist in higher numbers because they still did not enjoy equal economic opportunities. For his part, General Colin Powell rejected this argument. "The military," Powell noted, "had given African Americans more equal opportunity than any other institution in American society. But you cannot have it both ways—favoring opportunity for blacks in the military in peace-time and exemption from risk for them during wartime."

KEEPING THE COUNTRY SAFE

Today, racial and ethnic diversity in the U.S. armed forces is a given. Americans of all backgrounds have fought and died in the war in Afghanistan, which began in 2001. Americans of all backgrounds have fought and died in the war in Iraq, which began in 2003. Americans of all backgrounds continue to protect the nation against all potential threats.

In 1971, Samuel L. Gravely Jr. (1922–2004) became the first African American to achieve the rank of admiral in the U.S. Navy. Gravely had a distinguished 38-year career in the navy.

The advancement of African Americans to the rank of general or admiral is now routine. Togo West served as secretary of the army, that branch's top civilian post. Colin Powell served as the nation's highest-ranking military official, chairman of the Joint Chiefs of Staff.

Given these facts, it might seem natural to assume that race in the armed forces is no longer an issue at all. There are reasons to believe otherwise. A 2011 report commissioned by the U.S. Congress found that just 8 percent of the senior officers in the active-duty military were black. In contrast, 77 percent were white. So more progress needs be made.

Marcelite Harris (b. 1943) was the first African-American woman to reach the rank of general in the U.S. Air Force. When she retired from active duty in 1997, she was the highest-ranking woman in the American military.

American soldiers on patrol in the Wasit province of Iraq. As of 2012, more than 240,000 African Americans were actively serving in the American army, navy, air force, and marines, with another 130,000 serving in the national guard or as military reserves.

In the meantime, African Americans will continue to serve their country with distinction—as they have since the Revolutionary War. Major General Claude M. Bolton perfectly summed up African Americans' willingness to fight for their country, even when their country has not treated them very well. "This country is my country," said Bolton, a U.S. Force pilot who flew more than 230 combat missions in Vietnam and rose to the rank of major general.

My foreparents came here over 200 years ago. Though they were brought here in chains and shackles, they persevered and made this country and this land their home. With that in mind, it's not hard to understand why black men and women fought for this country. It's home and it's the only one that I truly know.

CHAPTER NOTES

p. 9:   "[General Powell] will bring leadership . . ." George H. W. Bush, "Remarks Announcing the Nomination of General Colin L. Powell to Be Chairman of the Joint Chiefs of Staff," August 10, 1989. http://www.presidency.ucsb.edu/ws/index.php?pid=17420

p. 9:   "without the sacrifices . . ." Colin Powell, quoted in Gail Buckley, *American Patriots: The Story of Blacks in the Military from the Revolution to Desert Storm* (New York: Random House, 2002), p. 443.

p. 10:   "brave and gallant soldier," Boston National Historical Park, "Salem Poor: 'A Brave and Gallant Soldier.'" http://www.nps.gov/bost/plany-ourvisit/upload/Salem%20Poor%202-14-01.pdf

p. 11:   "faithfully persevering . . ." Kareem Abdul-Jabbar and Alan Steinberg, *Black Profiles in Courage: A Legacy of African-American Achievement* (New York: HarperCollins, 2000), p. 31.

p. 13:   "I served in the Revolution . . ." Dr. Harris, quoted in Buckley, *American Patriots*, p. 3.

p. 15:   "I have yet to learn . . ." Isaac Chauncey, quoted in Michael Lee Lanning, *The African-American Soldier from Crispus Attucks to Colin Powell* (New York: Kensington Publishing, 2004), pp. 22–23.

p. 15:   "As sons of freedom . . ." Andrew Jackson, quoted in Lanning, *The African-American Soldier*, p. 24.

p. 15:   "I expected much from you . . ." Ibid., p. 25.

p. 17:   "I desire to inform you . . ." Jacob Dobson, quoted in Lanning, *The African-American Soldier*, p. 34.

p. 18:   "Colored men were good enough . . ." Frederick Douglass, quoted in James M. McPherson, *The Struggle for Equality* (Princeton, NJ: Princeton University Press, 1992), p. 193.

p. 19:   "They were exposed . . ." General Daniel Ullman, quoted in Lanning, *The African-American Soldier*, p. 41–42.

p. 21:   "No one but a member . . ." William Carney, quoted in Lanning, *The African-American Soldier*, p. 45.

p. 22:   "We must decide whether slavery . . ." Robert E. Lee, quoted in Michael Fellman, *The Making of Robert E. Lee* (Baltimore: The Johns Hopkins University Press, 2000) , p. 214.

p. 27:   "The troops are good . . ." Captain R. P. Hughes, quoted in Lanning, *The African-American Soldier*, p. 70.

p. 30: "I served in the infantry . . ." Major J. W. Wham, quoted in Lanning, *The African-American Soldier*, p. 76.

p. 34: "They were no braver . . ." Stephen Bonsal, quoted in Lanning, *The African-American Soldier*, p. 88.

p. 34: "brave men, worthy of respect . . ." Theodore Roosevelt, quoted in Lanning, *The African-American Soldier*, p. 91.

p. 41: "Inspired by Stowers' selfless . . ." Medal of Honor citation, quoted in Glenda Richardson, *Medal of Honor Recipients, 1979–2003* (Hauppauge, NY: Nova Science Publishers, 2003), p. 5.

p. 43: "We call upon the president . . ." *Pittsburgh Courier*, December 13, 1941. Quoted in Beth Bailey and David Farber, "The 'Double-V' Campaign in World War II Hawaii: African-Americans, Racial Ideology, and Federal Power," *Journal of Social History* (Summer 1993). http://findarticles.com/p/articles/mi_m2005/is_n4_v26/ai_14125267/

p. 44: "The Negro population . . ." Charles H. Houston, quoted in Lanning, *The African-American Soldier*, p. 162.

p. 46: "When the screaming . . ." *Birmingham News*, July 18, 1943, quoted in Lanning, *The African-American Soldier*, p. 194.

p. 48: "Men, you're the first . . ." George S. Patton, quoted in Buckley, *American Patriots*, p. 327.

p. 50: "It is hereby declared . . ." Executive Order 9981, quoted in Buckley, *American Patriots*, p. 339.

p. 53: "It doesn't make any difference . . ." Herbert M. Hart, quoted in Lanning, *The African-American Soldier*, p. 238.

p. 53: "A white man's war . . ." Dr. Martin Luther King Jr., quoted in Spencer C. Tucker, ed., *Encyclopedia of the Vietnam War: A Political, Social, and Military History* (Oxford, UK: ABC-CLIO, 1998), p. 9.

p. 54: "It was the most incredible display . . ." James Sanford, quoted in Catherine Reef, *African Americans in the Military* (New York: Fact On File, 2004), p. 153.

p. 54: "Through his bravery . . ." Medal of Honor citation, quoted in Jonathan Sutherland, *African Americans at War: An Encyclopedia* (Santa Barbara, CA: ABC-CLIO, 2004), p. 765.

p. 55: "The military had given . . ." Colin Powell, quoted in Lanning, *The African-American Soldier*, p. 285.

p. 57: "This country is my country . . ." Claude M. Bolton, quoted in Rudi Williams, "DoD Holds African American History Month Observance," American Forces Press Service, February 25, 2002. http://www.defense.gov/news/newsarticle.aspx?id=43908

CHRONOLOGY

1770   Former slave Crispus Attucks is the first person to die in the Boston Massacre on March 5.

1812–15   Black soldiers and sailors fight against the British in the War of 1812.

1861–65   Almost 200,000 African-American soldiers serve in black regiments during the Civil War.

1866   The U.S. Army creates six regiments of black soldiers; they are given the nickname Buffalo Soldiers. The number of Buffalo Soldier regiments will later be reduced to four.

1877   Henry O. Flipper becomes the first African American to graduate from the United States Military Academy at West Point.

1917–18   During World War I, more than 400,000 African Americans serve in the U.S. military in noncombat roles. Several African-American regiments are reassigned to fight in France's army, where they earn distinction.

1941–45   During World War II, more than a million African Americans serve in the U.S. armed forces, in segregated units.

1948   On July 26, President Harry S. Truman signs Executive Order 9981. It ends segregation in the U.S. military.

1950–53   During the Korean War, blacks and whites fight side by side in desegregated American combat units.

1965–73   During the Vietnam War, 20 African Americans earn the Medal of Honor.

1989   Colin Powell becomes the first African-American chairman of the Joint Chiefs of Staff.

1991   100,000 African-American men and women fight in the Persian Gulf War.

2001   Colin Powell becomes the first African American to serve as U.S. secretary of state. The war in Afghanistan begins.

2003   The Iraq War begins.

2011   A congressional report finds that just 8 percent of the senior officers in the active-duty military are African American.

GLOSSARY

abolitionist—a person who opposed slavery.

battalion—an army unit (typically 300 to 1,000 men) that is larger than a company but smaller than a brigade.

brigade—an army unit (typically 3,000 to 5,000 men) that is larger than a battalion but smaller than a division.

discrimination—the act of treating some people better than others for an unfair reason like race or ethnic background.

enlist—to join the armed forces as a volunteer.

integrate—to open something to people of all races, without any restrictions.

militia—a group of citizens who train to fight in an emergency but are not part of the regular army.

plantation—a large farm or estate, on which is usually grown a single crop.

racism—discrimination or prejudice based on a person's race; the belief that one race of people is superior to another.

rank—an official position or grade in the military.

recruits—new members of the armed forces.

regiment—a military unit made up of two or more battalions.

segregate—to separate or set apart one group of people from others.

squadron—in the air force, a group of airplanes organized in a unit.

FURTHER READING

Allen, Thomas B. *Harriet Tubman, Secret Agent: How Daring Slaves and Free Blacks Spied for the Union During the Civil War.* Washington, DC: National Geographic Children's Books, 2008.

Earl, Sari. *Benjamin O. Davis, Jr.: Air Force General & Tuskegee Airmen Leader.* Minneapolis: Abdo Publishing, 2010.

Hook, Sue Vander. *Colin Powell: General & Statesman.* Minneapolis: Abdo Publishing, 2010.

Myers, Walter Dean, and Bill Miles. *The Harlem Hellfighters: When Pride Met Courage.* New York: HarperCollins, 2005.

Raatma, Lucia. *African-American Soldiers in the Revolutionary War.* Minneapolis: Compass Point Books, 2008.

Stewart, Gail B. *Fighting for Freedom: Blacks in the American Military.* Farmington Hills, MI: Lucent Books, 2006.

INTERNET RESOURCES

http://www.buffalosoldierjr.com/

The kids' section of the official website of the Buffalo Soldiers National Museum in Houston, Texas, includes history, games, coloring sheets, and teacher materials about the Buffalo Soldiers.

http://www.nationalmuseum.af.mil/factsheets/factsheet.asp?id=1356

National Museum of the U.S. Air Force website, with information about the Tuskegee Airmen.

http://www.defense.gov/home/features/2007/blackhistorymonth/index.html

United States Department of Defense website for the history of African Americans in the military includes information, links, and photos.

http://www.pbs.org/wgbh/aia/part2/2narr4.html

This page, part of the online materials accompanying the PBS documentary series *Africans in America*, focuses on blacks during the Revolutionary War.

INDEX

Numbers in **bold italics** refer to captions.

CONTRIBUTORS

MARCIA AMIDON LUSTED has written more than 50 books for young readers, as well as hundreds of magazine articles. She is also an assistant editor for Cobblestone Publishing's six magazines, as well as a writing instructor and musician. She lives in New Hampshire with her family.

Senior Consulting Editor **DR. MARC LAMONT HILL** is one of the leading hip-hop generation intellectuals in the country. Dr. Hill has lectured widely and provides regular commentary for media outlets like NPR, the *Washington Post*, *Essence Magazine*, the *New York Times*, CNN, MSNBC, and *The O'Reilly Factor*. He is the host of the nationally syndicated television show *Our World With Black Enterprise*. Dr. Hill is a columnist and editor-at-large for the *Philadelphia Daily News*. His books include the award-winning *Beats, Rhymes, and Classroom Life: Hip-Hop Pedagogy and the Politics of Identity* (2009).

Since 2009 Dr. Hill has been on the faculty of Columbia University as Associate Professor of Education at Teachers College. He holds an affiliated faculty appointment in African American Studies at the Institute for Research in African American Studies at Columbia University.

Since his days as a youth in Philadelphia, Dr. Hill has been a social justice activist and organizer. He is a founding board member of My5th, a non-profit organization devoted to educating youth about their legal rights and responsibilities. He is also a board member and organizer of the Philadelphia Student Union. Dr. Hill also works closely with the ACLU Drug Reform Project, focusing on drug informant policy. In addition to his political work, Dr. Hill continues to work directly with African American and Latino youth.

In 2005, *Ebony* named Dr. Hill one of America's 100 most influential Black leaders. The magazine had previously named him one of America's top 30 Black leaders under 30 years old.